A coming out story...

Queer

A coming out story at almost age 40

Andrea G. Hardeman, M.S

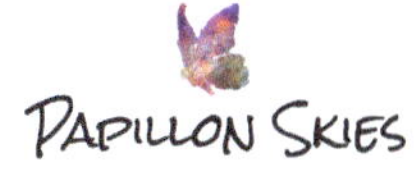

PAPILLON SKIES

Catalogued in-publication information is available from U.S. Library of Congress and Archives

ISBN (paperback): 979-8-9874070-0-4
ISBN (ebook): 979-8-9874070-1-1

First paperback edition 2023

Image Contributors: Mitch Hughes
Artwork, Illustrations, and Photographs: Andrea G. Hardeman
Interior design by Sophie Hanks
Cover design by Andrea G. Hardeman and Sheenah Freitas

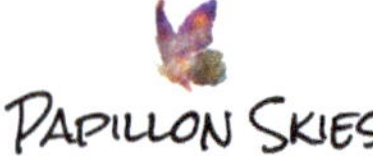

Papillon Skies
PapillonSkies.com

to all the queers

& those who love them

In hindsight the awakening
to my queerness grew
slowly

and started
when I tapped into
flow via painting in 2020.
It all came to a head through
poetry, and of course,
more painting.

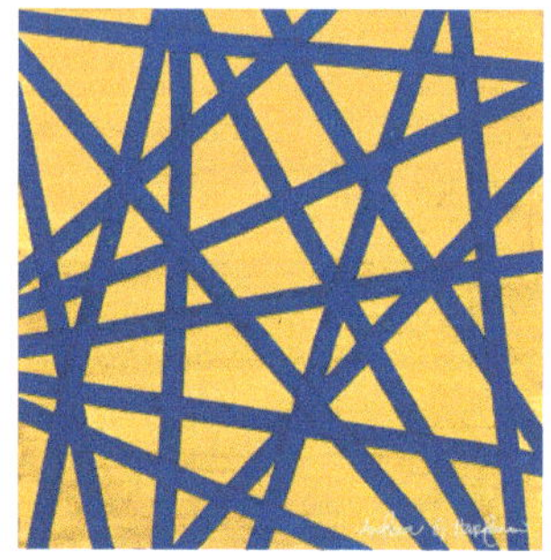

Trapped or Free, 2020. Mixed Media.

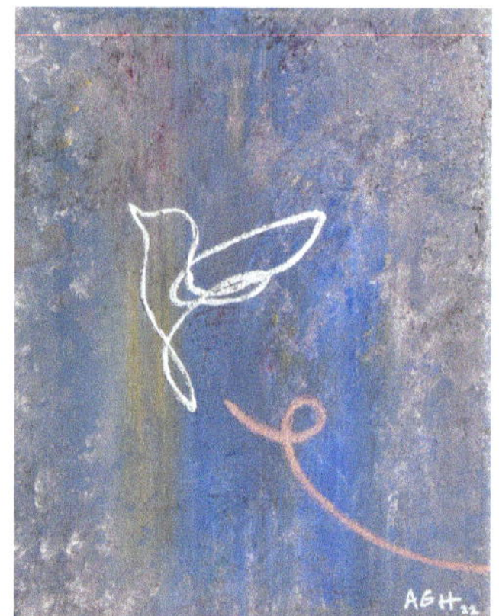

Free, 2022. Mixed Media.

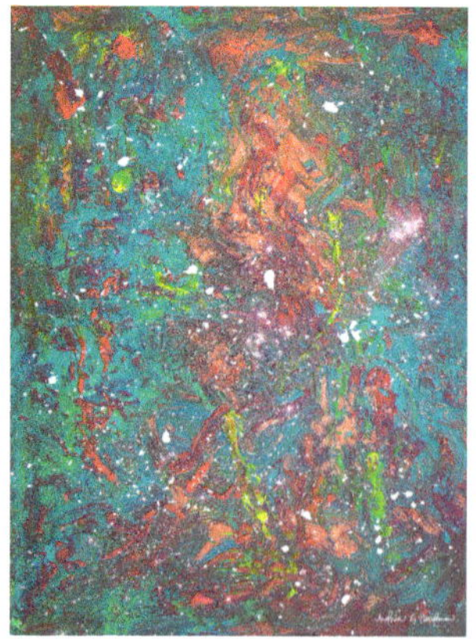

Here and Queer, 2022. Mixed Media.

I.

I casually reviewed my art pieces while working on this book and realized that my subconscious began preparing me to come out when I created *Trapped or Free* in 2020. *Trapped or Free* was an accidental painting that veered from my original plan. The notion behind the painting is that you don't know if you're inside the lined cage looking out or looking into the cage of lines. It's for the viewer to decide. If you're inside, then you're in a gilded cage. And if you're outside, it could be that your desire (represented by the gold inside the cage) feels out of reach. Not realizing I am queer for practically four decades was a gilded cage for me.

II.

I painted *Free* shortly before coming out, and it represents beginning your journey toward freedom and being in a general forward motion. Creating art lowkey propelled me on my identity journey.

III.

August 5-7 was the weekend I came out to myself. I felt overwhelmed and unsure. There was internal resistance to accepting being queer. Painting had become a trusted friend by this time, so I laid everything I was feeling inside onto the canvas. I felt drawn to the neon colors, which turned out to be symbolic throughout my self-discovery process. Painting *Here and Queer* was a clear confirmation to me of my queerness in a way that I could no longer deny.

here

not everyone queer
shouts, "hell yeah, i'm
here." some slowly bloom
to an awakening in fear.

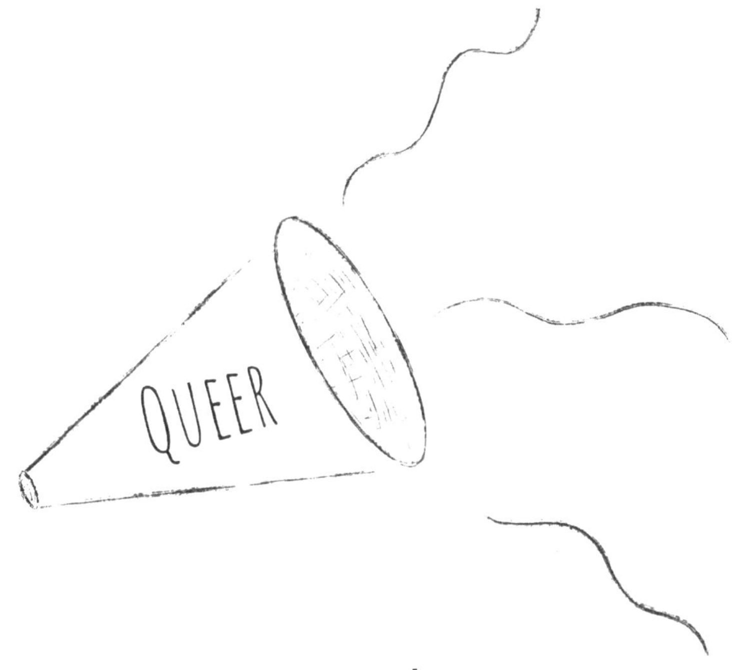

RE: Below Her Mouth

My thoughts: Can't a girl just like a lesbian flick with erotic scenes and not be gay?

February 2020

Me: I have this movie that I'm obsessed with and don't know who would watch it with me. Want to watch it?

Alyx [post movie]: Are you sure you're not queer?

Me: Yep. Pretty sure. I'm just an ally.

August 5, 2022

Me: I really love the movie Below Her Mouth.

Tess: You are so gay!

Me [nervous smile]: Two of my queer friends asked me if I was sure I'm not queer. I just really love the movie.
...

Me: I really love Kristen Stewart's style and want to find similar clothes.

Tess [smirks]

Me: What was that face for?

Tess: That's a very queer style.

Me [shrug]: I really like the clothes.

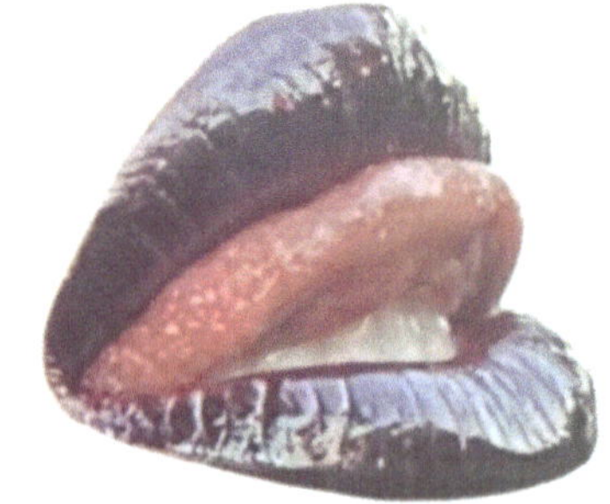

that will do it

when he told
me that my
solar plexus
and heart
chakras were
closed i couldn't
comprehend
a reason. after all,
i had found my
voice and had
been embracing
my truth.

a few days after
coming out
to myself and
leaning into
my truth my
muscles re-aligned
with those chakras
and loosened for the
first time in decades.
my truth had energetically
burrowed itself and pulled
my muscles taut to
protect my internal
organs in an act of
protection and survival.
The muscle tensions
promptly released once
i acknowledged and
began embodying my truth.

Initial thoughts
while wrapping my mind around coming out

I feel like I'm walking through
someone else's dream.

I want time to stand still,
so I can tackle one thing at a time.

I'd like to unsubscribe
from this major life change.

I need a queer trainer.

reconcile

i fear the moment
of reckoning is here

looking back
the image of
Matthew Shepard
was always near

his death engendered a fear that
overshadowed my inner knowing—

masking

how i have always been queer
and all the subtle breadcrumbs
i had wandered past over the years

oh, dear.

another major life
transition is here
take a fucking #
i'm working over here

Kicking ass and
taking names
leading and
delegating while
charging toward
my goals

can't stop
won't stop
shit happens
and golly wow
now i'm queer

fan-fucking-tastic

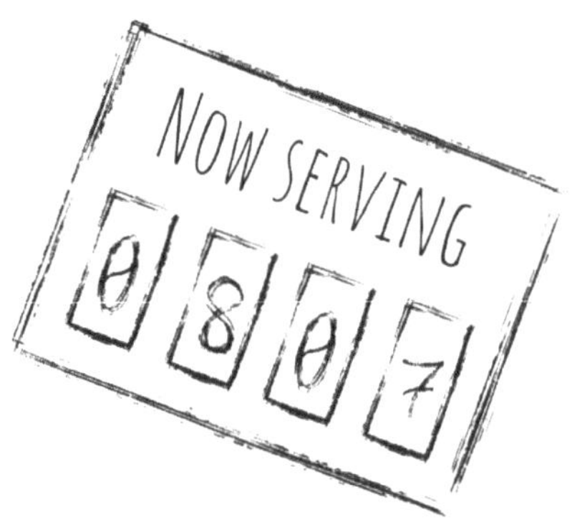

emotional roller coaster

i ride a
roller coaster
with tracks lined
in fear and titillation
with each ascent, and on
the downward sprint
i am filled with
elation.

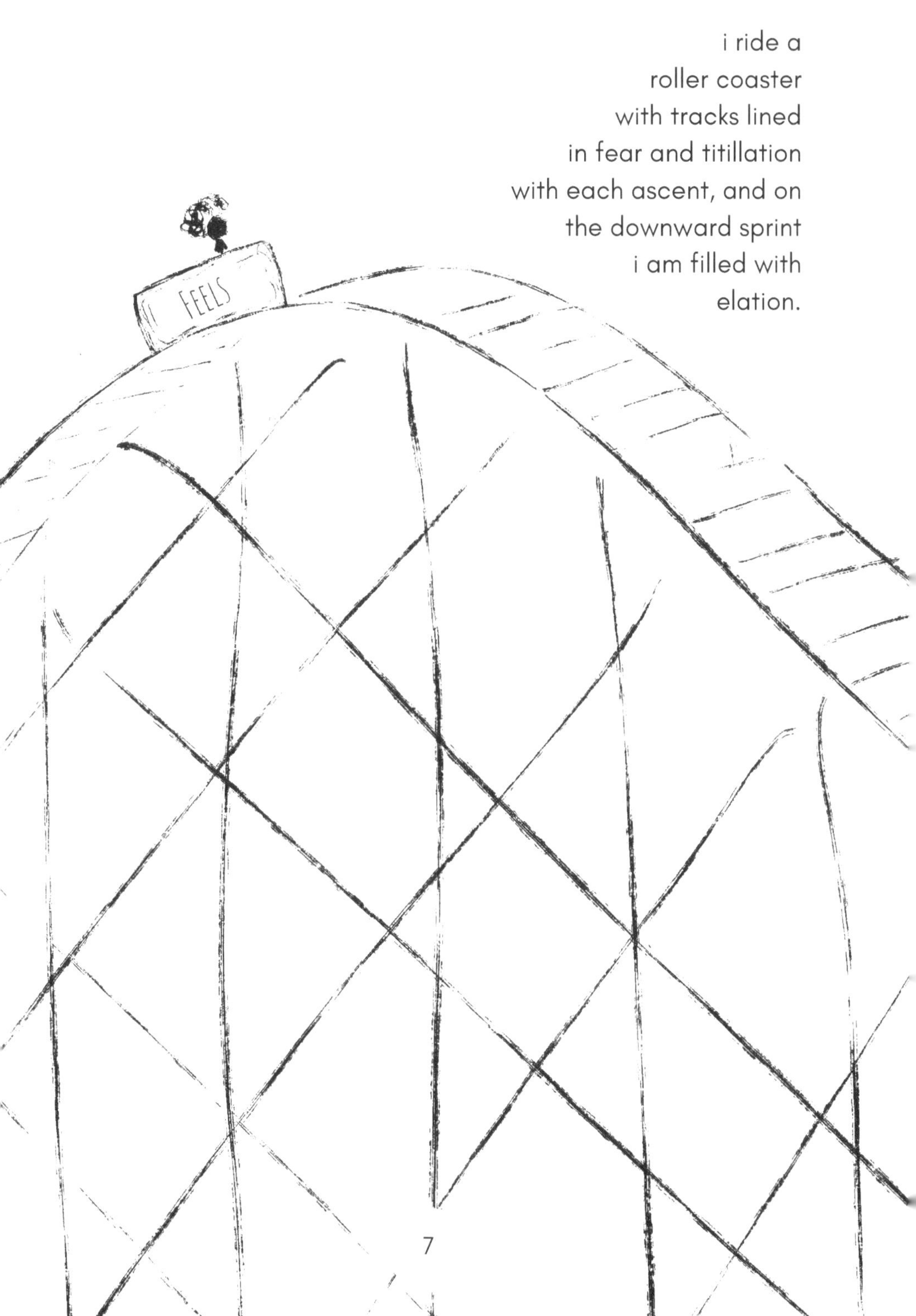

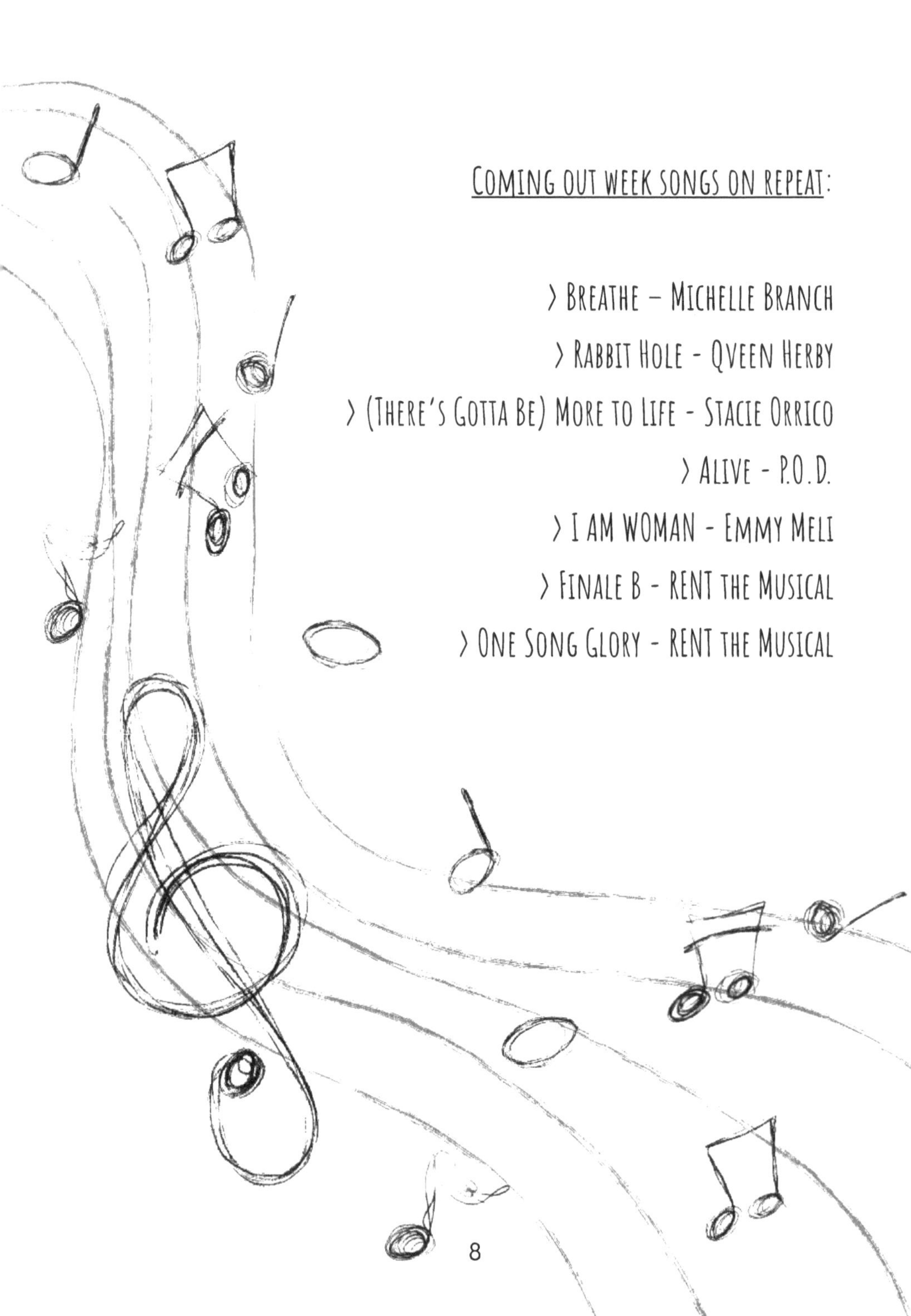

Coming out week songs on repeat:

> Breathe – Michelle Branch
> Rabbit Hole - Qveen Herby
> (There's Gotta Be) More to Life - Stacie Orrico
> Alive - P.O.D.
> I AM WOMAN - Emmy Meli
> Finale B - RENT the Musical
> One Song Glory - RENT the Musical

Reckoning.

It feels like a dream
that's happening to
someone else. This
coming to terms
with my queer self.

Losing your dad

My brother
lost our father
the moment he
embraced his truth.
Daddy told him,
"No one will want you
around their children."

I remember passively
thinking over the years
that my parents can't
have two gay kids. It
didn't seem fair to
shatter their dreams
of who and what we could
be. With that being settled,
there was no way that I, too,
could be any shade of gay.

Even if I never tell our
father, our relationship
remains the same—
sporadic and distant.
To tell him is to potentially
lose him completely. We're
in a different time, but I
have no way of knowing
if he stayed standing in
the same place and let
the world pass him by.

path to queer

i don't want
to be here on
this path i
didn't choose

is how i felt
at the start
of my coming
out week which
felt like a whole
damn year

looking back
it was inevitable
that i'd end up
standing here

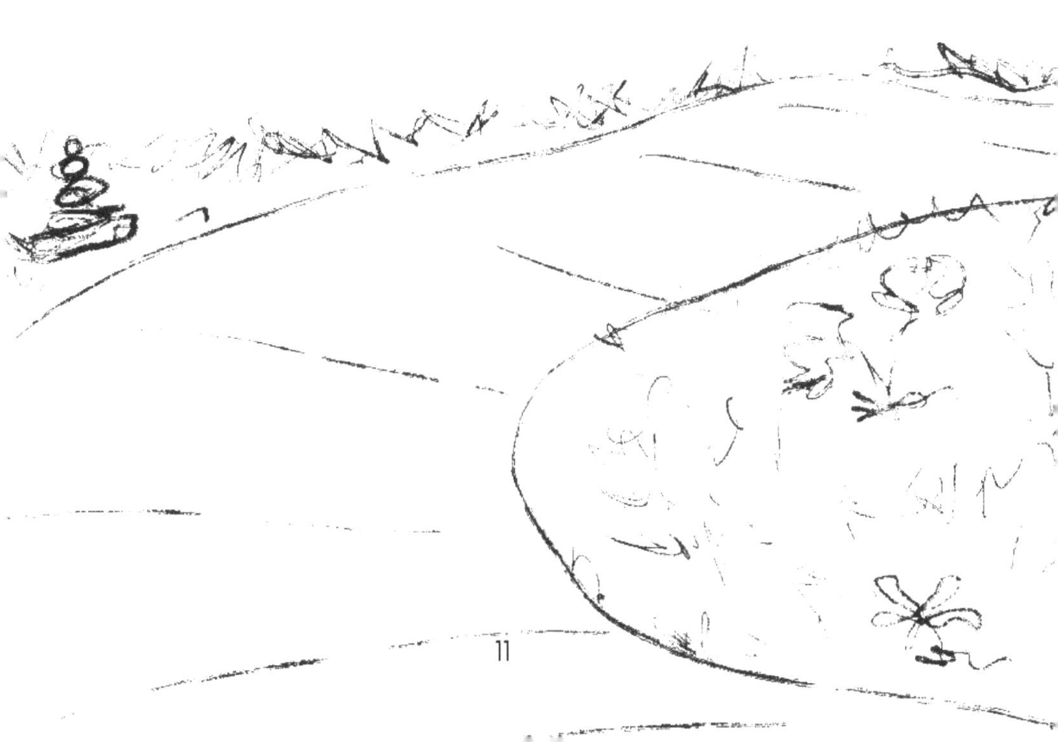

11

>>here<<

they loved someone
i never truly knew
tho she looked
and spoke like me

with an imprisoned mind
she was never fully free

will they now accept
every which way
i tend to be

Clothes

I feel free
from the
male gaze—
now able to
dress in all
the gender
queer ways

I mostly
conformed
to norms
by way of
semi-dressy
but mostly
casual tomboy
femme arrays

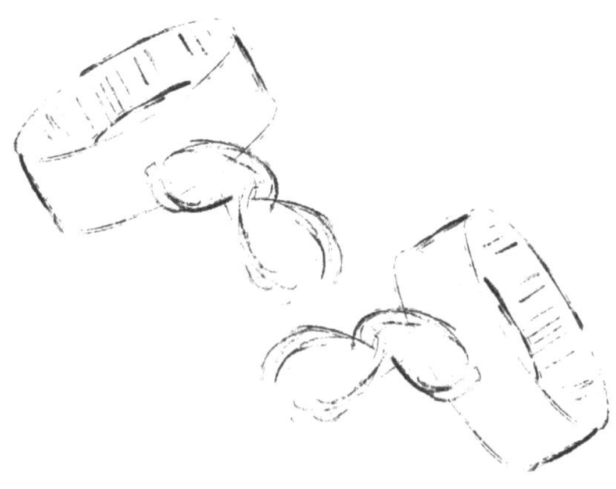

Question

Mother,
will you
love this
queer
version
of me?

I'd
rather
not be
abandoned
emotionally.

answer

and-dree-uh,
why would u
think that?

i don't but i
just need to
hear u say it.

i am not him
nor will i ever
be, sweetie, u
r stuck with me.

P.S. My mom and brother always say my name
with this particular emphasis when making a point
or calling me out. This is not the correct
pronunciation of my name.

QuEer

I vacillate
between
excitement
and fear
to tell the
world that I
am queer

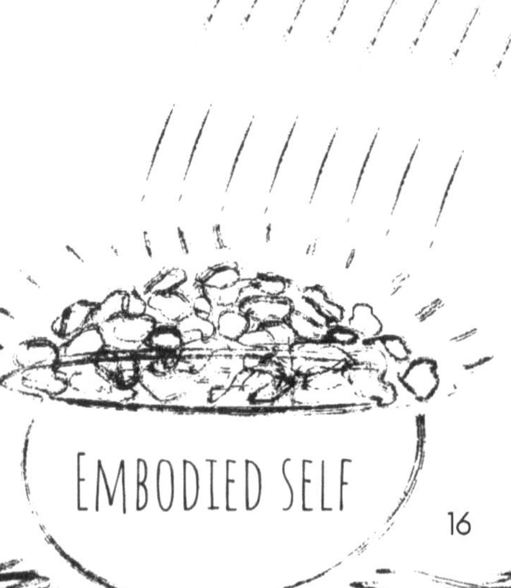

16

fear

It's not queer that I fear
the slight or unsuspecting
jeer that hits with a hard hook,
when you look like you drew
outside the lines arbitrarily
prescribed to your presenting
chromosomes. It's by way of
design to keep everyone in
line like Stepford Wives.
Under sedation by mass
marketing manipulation,
media, and by the way things
have "always" been. We're sold
to without consent, lulled into
submission, and blinded by
division. When in reality, we
all come from the same source
and meet the same end—from
ashes to ashes, dust to dust.

unboxing

i like girls
i like boys
androgynous
femmes and
tomboys

i have had
secret crushes
on them all

the ways

I'm amazed
by all the ways
I played to the
male gaze—
tangled up in a
spider's web and
bound tightly with
silken threads of
stereotypes steeped
in compulsory
heteronormativity.

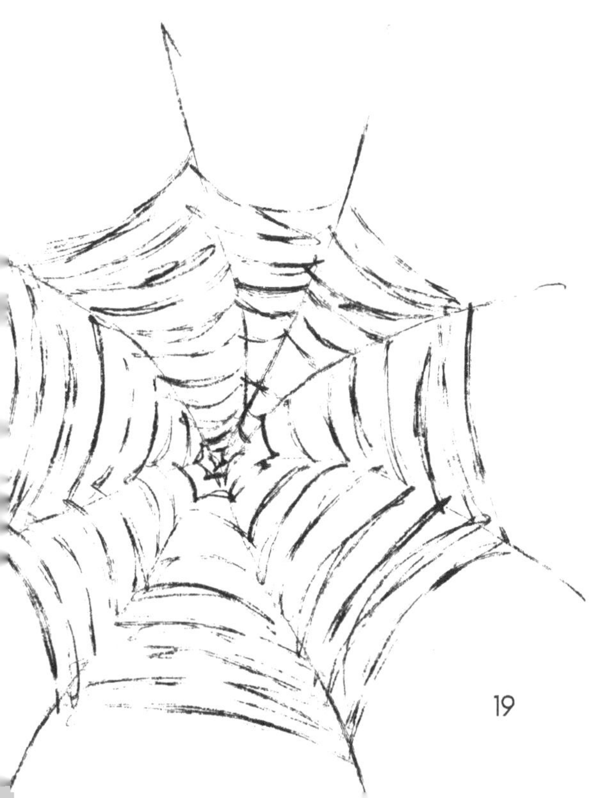

19

Q

Q is for queer
and soft butch
lips and tongues
and for finally
feeling at one

The writer of
Below Her Mouth
responds to my
comment.

And...

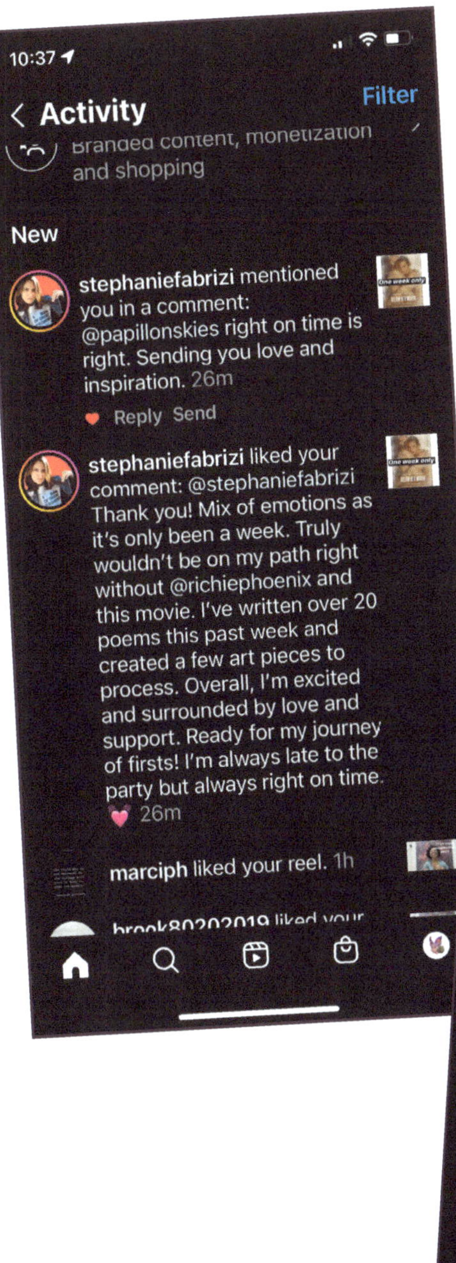

Erika Linder,
the lead actress,
likes my comment.

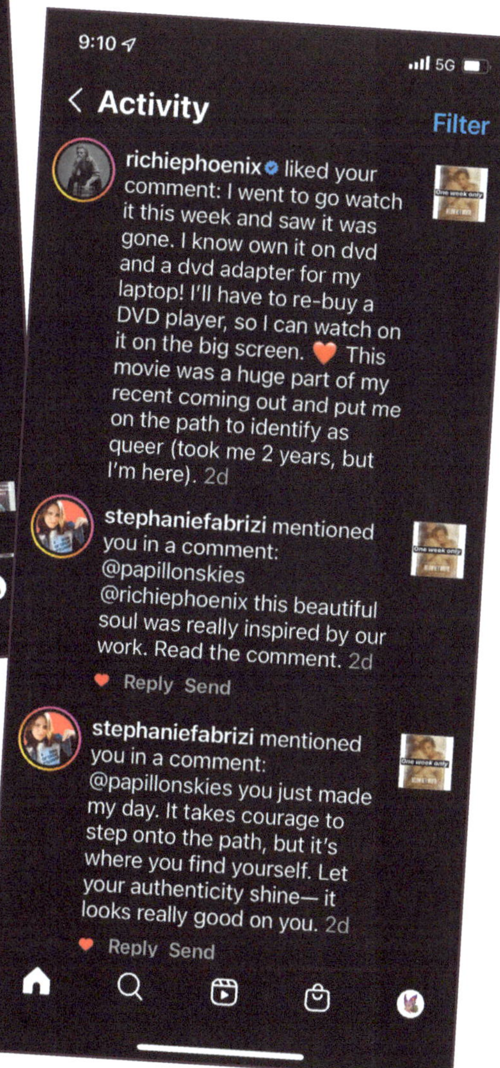

Evolve

Nothing
in this
world is
in a static
state, so
why freak
out during
an active
internal
change?

acceptance

finally free
to embrace
the queer me
and good lawd
what a sight
she is to see

how i knew

she wasn't the match
but rather the last
motion of the strike
that lit the flame

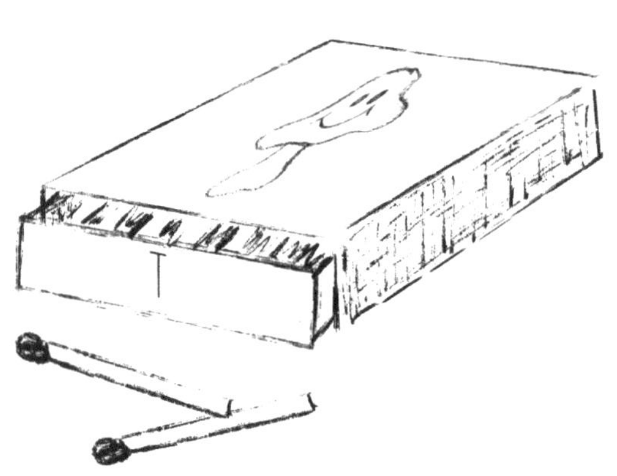

my interpretation

What does being
queer mean to me?

It means fuck the
male gaze and
the patriarchy!

It means that I am
finally free to examine,
to exhume, and finally
discover how it feels to
live more dynamically.

crush

she was the first
time that i allowed
myself to feel the rush
and acknowledge that
i have a bonified
female crush

she was the first
time i realized that
i could be free to
love a woman

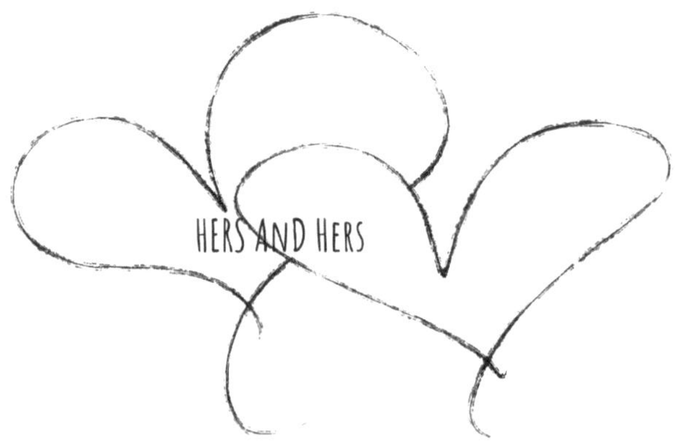

new beginnings

it's as though i'm seeing the colors
of a sunrise for the first time.

today there's a magnificent blue
paired with a deep pink hue.

it's the coming of the dawn
after a long metaphorical night.

it's like the advent of technicolor
after only knowing black and white.

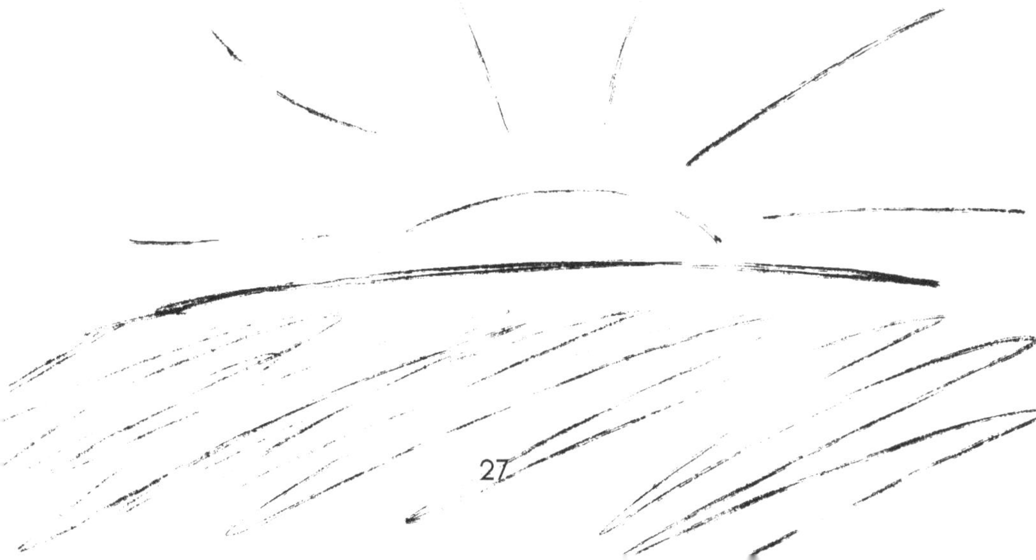

slow bloom

The florist
still loves
those who
are slow
to bloom.

They
anticipate
and appreciate
each majestic bloom.

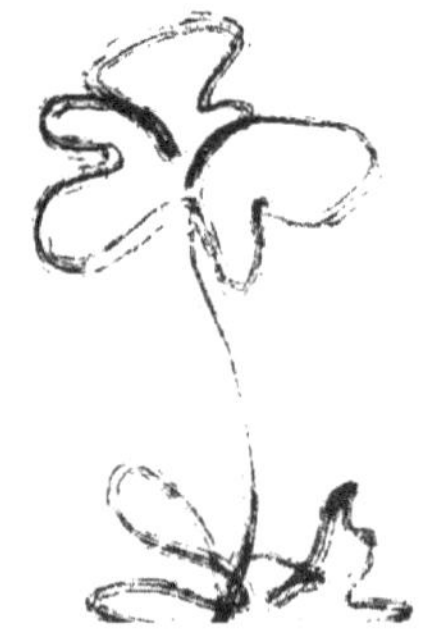

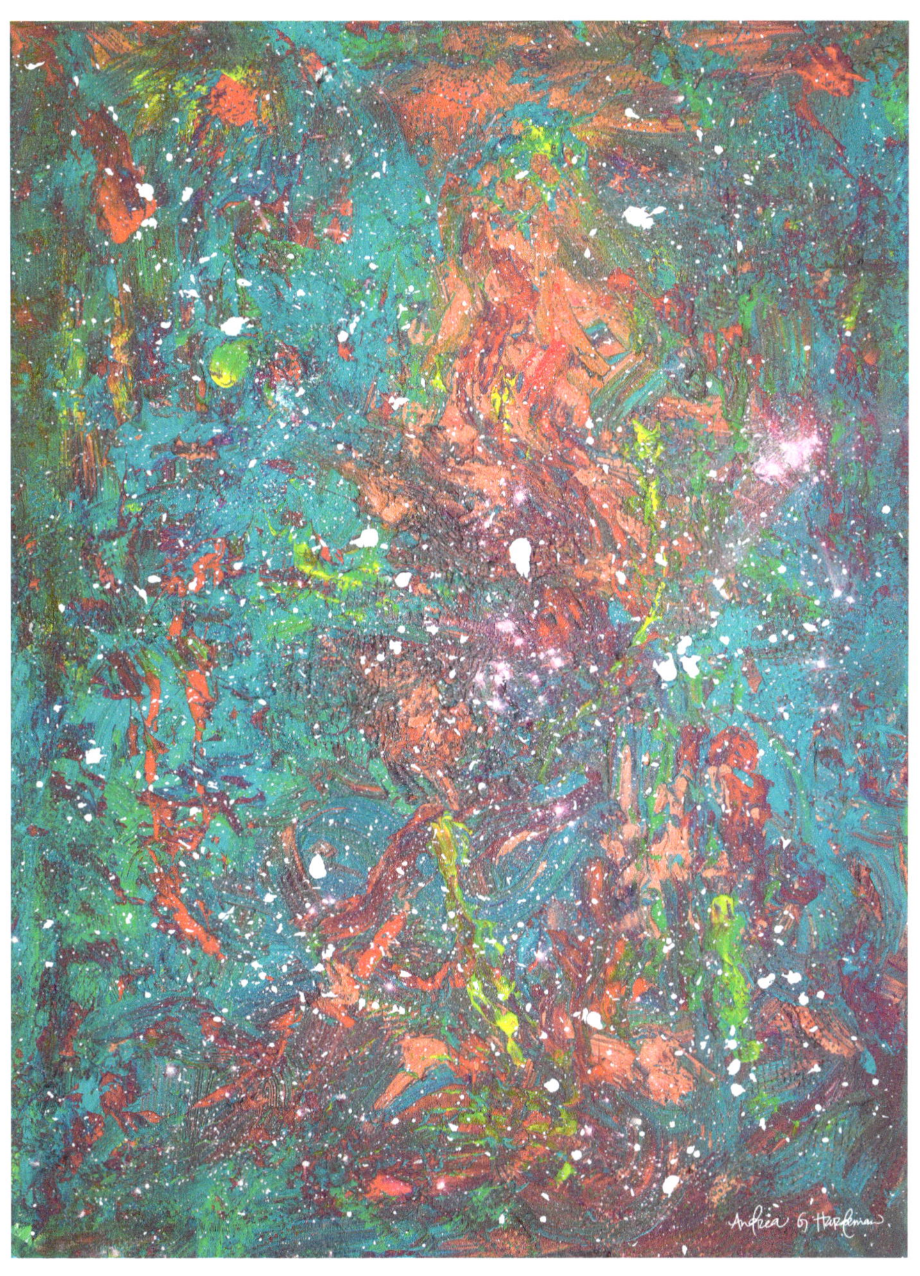

Here and Queer, 2022. Mixed Media.

You are worthy.
You are seen.
You are loved.
Your voice matters.
Your feelings are valid.

Stay;